NATIONAL GEOGRAPHIC

T0045279

My Family Tree

Marvin Buckley

My name is Will.
I am making a family tree.
I am seven years old.
I've lived in the same town all my life.

Will

Can you see me on my family tree?

3

This is my little sister, Liz.
She is five years old.
She started school this year.
She was born in the same place as me.

Will

Liz

Can you *see* my sister on my family tree?

5

This is my mom.
She was born a long time ago.
She moved here twelve years ago.
She moved here to get a job.

Mom

Will

Liz

Can you *see* my mom
on my family tree?

This is my dad.
He has lived in this town his entire life.
He met my mom after she moved here.
They got married ten years ago.

Mom

Dad

Will

Liz

Can you see my dad on my family tree?

These are my grandparents.
I call them Grandma and Grandpa.
They are my mom's mom and dad.
They live far away in another state.

Grandma Grandpa

Mom Dad

Will Liz

Can you see my grandma and grandpa on my family tree?

11

These are my other grandparents.
They are my dad's mom and dad.
I call them Nana and Pop.
They live nearby.

Grandma Grandpa Nana Pop

Mom Dad

Will Liz

Can you *see* Nana and Pop on my family tree?

13

My Family Tree

This is my family tree.
My grandparents, parents, sister,
and I are on my family tree.
My family tree tells the story of
my family.

Grandma Grandpa Nana Pop

Mom Dad

Will Liz

Every family has a different family tree. Who would you put on your family tree?